Contents

Introduction

Just as the *Foundations* Guided Reading Books aim to provide closely structured support through which children can build up their skills in reading, the activity sheets aim to support the links between Reading and Speaking and Listening, as well as between Reading and Writing.

Their aim is to provide opportunities for guided writing and guided discussion through a series of activities whose preparation can be carried out as a class or as a group, with the help of a teacher, teaching assistant or parent, and in which children can work as independently as possible.

The format of the sheets

Each activity page has three sections:
● Part A
● Parts B/C
● Notes for guidance.

Part A

This activity is usually linked directly to the Guided Reading Books following the theme or events from the story.

Activities in A often require the children to find the specific information or vocabulary and are designed to check the children's understanding of what the book is about.

Observation of children while they complete these sheets as end of book activities in the classroom will provide teachers with valuable information about their progress.

Part B/C

These activities aim to support children in extending and applying knowledge from each book. Often they take the theme of the story and link it to the children's own experience.

Some activities give the children opportunities for language play or to try out their own developing skills as writers on the theme of the book. Many are intended to add a little fun.

Notes for guidance

At the bottom of each page there are simple notes giving guidance on the activities for parents or carers. More detailed information is given in the Lesson Plan for each Guided Reading Book in the *Teacher's Guide to Using the Reading Books* for each stage. Where appropriate, guidance is given for children of different abilities.

Each activity sheet in the *Foundations for Reading Scheme* requires the child to return to the Guided Reading Book for information. They are not intended as simply copy-and-draw activities.

Where children are asked to find particular words or phrases from the book, it is anticipated that they begin, even at this very early level, to develop the 'look and cover and write and check' approach. Children should be encouraged to hold at least a syllable at a time in their minds rather than copying words letter by letter.

The development of good habits such as these is a vital part of the **Foundations Strategic Teaching Approach**.

For this reason, it is recommended, at least in the early stages, that the children are organised as a class or in groups for completing the sheets.

Strategy	Behaviour
Directionality	Children use fingers to indicate direction and return (left to right).
One-to-one matching	Children begin to match one spoken word with one written word.

Activities in part A

The activities on part A of the sheets link directly to each of the Guided Reading Books. They should be completed with reference to the individual books. Children are not expected to memorise the book or guess at answers, but rather to use the book itself as a source of information on which to base and check their answers and as a stimulus for their independent writing. This is part of the *Foundations* philosophy of developing strong links between reading and writing. The habits of scanning, pinpointing and checking information at this early level will prepare the children for using books as sources of information and research as they develop as readers and writers.

Activities in part A include:

- **Cloze activities** – completing sentences by finding missing words or phrases from the Guided Reading Books.
- **Labelling** – providing labels for items, people or specific vocabulary.
- **Illustrating** – not simply drawing a picture, but illustrating events or episodes from the story to show detail and understanding of what the story was about.
- **Retelling** – presenting events from the story in a different way, perhaps using a different sentence structure, turning simple sentences into continuous prose or changing the format into a table or list.
- **Literal comprehension** – answering simple 'Yes' or 'No' questions to show understanding of the plot.

The second part of each activity sheet is intended to broaden and extend the knowledge gained from the Guided Reading Books in one of four ways:

- **Retelling** – taking the theme from the book and developing it in a different way. This vital early activity is built into each *Foundations* lesson as one of the most effective ways of checking children's understanding. The activity sheets present this in different ways, encouraging children to explore different types of writing such as lists, writing letters or giving instructions. (See individual Lesson Plans for more details.)

- **Relating** – linking the plot or theme of the Guided Reading Book to the experience of the children themselves. A keeping fit theme in the Guided Reading Book might be used to encourage the children to recount their own experiences of sport.

- **Reflective language play** – these activities are included primarily for fun, but it is hoped that as the children enjoy them they will learn about the rhythms and patterns of language and add to their knowledge of how language works. This play often indicates that the children are gaining confidence and are able to take control.

- **Development of phonological awareness** – the activities in part B often require children to 'try out' their developing knowledge of some of the patterns and strings within words. (See the *Teacher's Handbook* and the *Teacher's Guide to Using the Reading Books* for more details.)

Using the activity sheets in the classroom

Each sheet is closely linked to a Guided Reading Book and children will need a copy of the appropriate book to complete the activities.

They have been set out as separate sheets that allow them to be used as part of a daily lesson from *Foundations*. Although teachers may wish to clip several sheets together for ease of organisation, they are not intended as workbooks. The sheets are not designed for children to work through as 'busy work'.

Following class or group work on the Guided Reading Book, it is intended that the teacher or helper should prepare the children for the activity sheet before they begin working independently. Some teachers might prefer to make an enlarged A3 version of the sheet so that the children can work on it in groups before completing their own individual sheets.

The Extension activities might also be completed by groups of children with the support of a classroom assistant or volunteer helper. There are more detailed notes on how classroom assistants might give support in the *Teacher's Handbook* and the *Teacher's Guide to Using the Reading Books*.

The table on the opposite page is designed to help teachers to use the activity sheets as part of a *Foundations* guided lesson.

Using the activity sheets as part of a Foundations Guided Reading Lesson

Class/group collaborative work

Working through the Guided Reader.
Discussion of the plot and themes.
Reading the book together.
Focusing on characters, plot or language.

Approximately 20 mins.

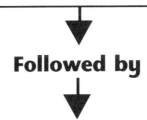

Followed by

Class/group preparation for Class or Home activity sheets

Working through activity sheet (A3) children
volunteer answers to each part.
Teacher gives guidance on organisation:
- work in class or at home
- work independently or in pairs
- work immediately on sheets or after supplementary activity.

Approximately 10 mins.

Children work:

Independently on part A.

Approximately 10–20 mins.

High frequency word reinforcement activities and games
Approximately 10–20 mins.

Phonic development activities and games

Approximately 10–20 mins.

Children work:

Independently on part B and C (when it occurs).
On part B/C at home as homework.
Independently on extended work with the Guided Reading Book.
On other work designated by the teacher.

Approximately 10–20 mins.

FOUNDATIONS FOR READING – *Homework Activities for Early Readers*

Using the activity sheets at home

Where teachers prefer, the activity sheets might also be used, in whole or part, as homework sheets for parents to complete with their children. The children will need the Guided Reading Books to complete the sheets, which might be completed after they have read each book to or with their parents.

Teachers may wish to use the sheets in two parts. Part A provides an opportunity to observe and monitor children's progress. Following this the children, after some guided discussion and preparation, could work at their own pace through part B or complete it at home.

Where the activity sheets are used at home they can provide parents with constant feedback on the children's progress. They provide opportunities for parents to be more closely involved in themes on which their children are working in school.

The notes for guidance on each activity sheet are intended to be used by either teaching assistants, volunteer helpers or parents with a minimum of extra support from teachers.

More information and details on involving parents in the *Foundations for Reading Scheme* are given in each teacher's guide.

Making Things

A Join the correct face to what they made.

Carlos

beds

toys

Nick

Carmen

biscuits

earrings

Paulo

B Fill in the missing words.

Nick is my
_____ .

Paulo is my
_____ .

Carmen is my
_____ .

Carlos is my
_____ .

Extension activities (delete before photocopying or leave as instructions for parents or carers).
A. The children should draw lines to link the characters to the things that they made. Ask them to try this without looking back at the book, then to check their answers using the book.
B. The children should complete the speech bubbles so that the characters describe people in the family. Ask the children what the characters in the book make things from, for example: toys – wood.

FOUNDATIONS FOR READING – *Homework Activities for Early Readers*

Mum's New Car

A Colour the cars.

a red car

a blue car

a green car

B Fill in the missing words.

Pete liked the _____ _____ .

Maria liked the _____ _____ .

Uncle Joe said, "Do you want a

_____ _____ ?"

C Fill in the missing words.

new	old

Mum said, "My car is _____ .

I need a _____ one."

Extension activities (delete before photocopying or leave as instructions for parents or carers).
A. Draw the children's attention to the designs of the cars – each one is different. They should colour the cars.
B. The children should fill in the missing words (the cars from part A).
C. Ask the children what Mum said when she found the car she liked and what Uncle Joe, Pete and Maria said.

The Big Sneeze

A Fill in the missing words.

> the dog   Jan   Dad   Kelly   the cat   Mum   Pat

Jan's big sneeze hits _____ .

Pat's big sneeze hits _____ .

Kelly's big sneeze hits _____ .

Mum's big sneeze hits _____ .

Dad's huge sneeze hits _____ ,

_____ and _____ .

B Who has a cold?   ✔   or   ✗

the cat ☐   the dog ☐

Dad ☐   Mum ☐

Pat ☐   Kelly ☐

Jan ☐

Extension activities (delete before photocopying or leave as instructions for parents or carers).
A. The children should fill in the missing words and then read the sentences. They could draw the characters in order using arrows to show the journey of the sneeze.
B. Having ticked or crossed the characters, the children could draw those characters who did not sneeze.

Scratch My Back

A Fill in the missing words.

Mother   Baby

_____ Hippopotamus   _____ Hippopotamus

B Fill in the missing words.

Baby Hippopotamus scratched Mother Hippopotamus's _____.	back front
"_____ a little more," said Mother Hippopotamus.	Down Up
"That's _____," said Mother Hippopotamus.	good bad

Extension activities (delete before photocopying or leave as instructions for parents or carers).
A. The children should fill in the missing words and then read the completed captions, checking them against the pictures.
B. They should complete the sentences and then use the book to check their answers. Ask the children to find some things that scratch – they could draw and label them. Examples could include: nail file, emery board, back-scratcher, cat's claws, cheese-grater, pan scourer, stiff brush.

Where is the Milk?

A Fill in the missing words.

Matt and Jim went to the _____ .	park shop fair
They went to get the _____ .	milk sugar bread
The big boys were _____ _____ .	playing cards riding bikes playing games
Matt and Jim _____ .	played talked watched

B Put the words in the right order.

_____ _____ _____
_____

milk?

Where

the

is

Extension activities (delete before photocopying or leave as instructions for parents or carers).
A. The children should fill in the missing words to show what happened in the story. Provide cut-up copies of the activity for them to order the events of the story.
B. To put the words in the right order the children should look for the word that begins with a capital letter (this is the first word) and then the word that is followed by a question mark (this comes last). Ask the children what Dad said when Matt and Jim got home.

Snails

A Do snails eat these? ✔ or ✗

flowers ☐

jelly ☐

flies ☐

worms ☐

vegetables ☐

fish ☐

B Fill in the missing words.

Snails live in _____ .

Snails live in _____ .

Snails live in _____ .

Snails live on _____ .

Snails live on _____ .

Snails live under _____ .

houses

rocks

ponds

the sea

trees

the land

plants

gardens

Extension activities (delete before photocopying or leave as instructions for parents or carers).
A. The children should use the book to find out what snails eat, encouraging them to present the information in a different way (as a tick or a cross).
B. The children should fill in the missing words to show all the places where snails live. The activity reinforces the positional words 'in', 'on' and 'under'. Using the book or observing a real snail the children could make a drawing of a snail and label the parts that they know.

Guess What?

A Fill in the missing words. Draw a line from the objects to what they are used for.

| paper | pen | pencil | crayons |

write

make a book

colour

draw

B Fill in the missing words.

I write _____ with my pen.	pictures colours words
I read my _____ .	paper book pen
I draw _____ with my pencil.	pictures colour words
I _____ my pictures with my crayons.	

Baby Elephant's Sneeze

A Fill in the missing words.

Look at the _____.
That will stop the sneeze.

tissue

nose

light

Hold your _____.
That will stop the sneeze.

Get a _____,
quickly!

Dad

B | Yes | or | No |

Baby Elephant's nose was itchy. ☐

Mother Elephant said "Look at the light." ☐

Dad said "Have a drink." ☐

Baby Elephant sneezed "Aaaahhhhhhchooooooo!" ☐

Extension activities (delete before photocopying or leave as instructions for parents or carers).
A. Ask the children if they can remember what happened in the story. They should fill in the missing words then read the sentences that they have written. Encourage them to check their answers using the book.
B. The children may need to use the book to check what happened in the story. Ask the children what they would do if they were going to sneeze.

Mr Crawford

A Write what they said in the speech bubbles.

> Go and see.

> Hello, Mr Crawford.

> Why does Mr Crawford sit on the wall all day?

B Who said "Hello" to Mr Crawford? Write the names and draw the faces.

First ...	Then ...

Then ...	Then ...	Then ...

Extension activities (delete before photocopying or leave as instructions for parents or carers).
A. The children should copy the words into the correct speech bubbles to show what the characters in the story said.
B. The children should draw the people and write their names under the pictures. This activity could be cut up for the children to order the events in the story. Ask the children why they think Mr Crawford sat on the wall all day.

A Day Shopping

A What are they looking for? ✔

	music	chairs	clothes	watches	food	hats
sister						
grandpa						
dad						
mum						
brother						
grandma						

B Fill in the missing letters.
Use the pictures to help.

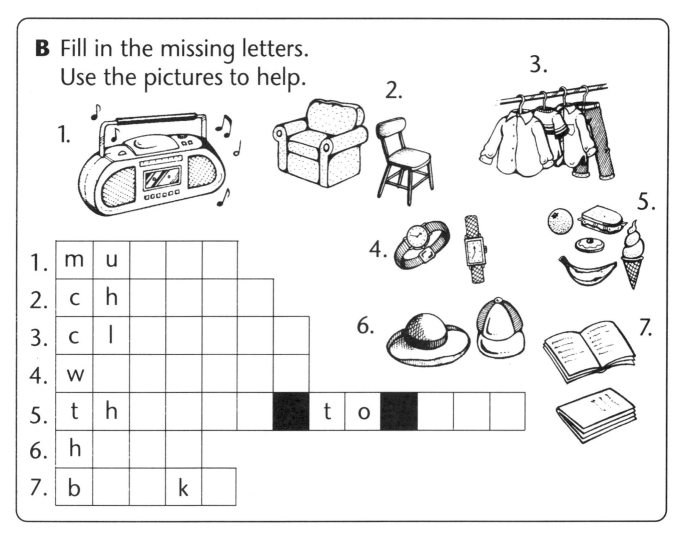

1. | m | u |
2. | c | h |
3. | c | l |
4. | w |
5. | t | h | | | | t | o |
6. | h |
7. | b | | | k |

Extension activities (delete before photocopying or leave as instructions for parents or carers).

A. Ask the children what each person was looking for in the shops. The activity encourages them to present this information using a chart. They should put a tick on the chart to show what each person was looking for.

B. The children could use the book or activity A to remind themselves of what the characters found at the shops. They should look at the pictures and then fill in the missing letters to make the words.

FOUNDATIONS FOR READING – *Homework Activities for Early Readers*

Where Can Teddy Go?

A What are they packing?
Draw lines to join the pictures.

 Dad

 Carrie

 Mum

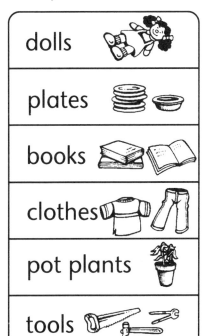

- dolls
- plates
- books
- clothes
- pot plants
- tools

 Gran

 Uncle Derek

 Rachel

B Finish the sentences.

BOOKS	Teddy will _____ _____ .	get squashed
Carrie's clothes	Teddy will _____ _____ .	get torn
Plants	Teddy will _____ _____ .	get dirty
Plates	Teddy will _____ _____ .	get lost
TOOLS	Teddy will _____ _____ .	get dusty

Extension activities (delete before photocopying or leave as instructions for parents or carers).
A. The children should use the story to find out what each character was packing and then draw a line between them and the correct objects.
B. Ask the children to explain why Teddy could not be packed with each character's things. They should fill in the missing words and then read what they have written. They could then draw a picture to show where Teddy did go.

Close Your Eyes

A Join the pictures to the correct words.

lion   needle   film

 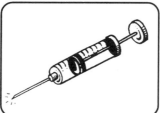 

(zoo)   (doctor)   (fair)   (dentist)   (pictures)

 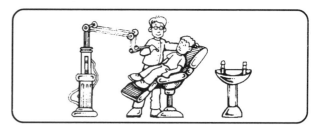

roller coaster   drill

B Answer the questions.

What can Danny do if he is scared of the lion?

_____

What can he do if he gets scared of the needle?

_____

What can Dad do if he gets scared of the film?

_____

Extension activities (delete before photocopying or leave as instructions for parents or carers).
A. The children should draw a line to join each thing to the place where Danny will see it.
B. They should write what Danny can do if these things scare him (close his eyes).
Ask the children to draw a picture to show something that scares them. They could give it a heading and write next to it what they can do when they are scared.

Farms

A Fill in the missing letters. Use the pictures to help.

1.

2.

1.	v		g		t		b	l	e	s
2.	c	r								
3.	f	r								
4.	c									

3.

4.

B Join the picture to the place it comes from.

orchard
dairy farm
cattle farm
mussel bed
wheat farm
market garden
sheep farm

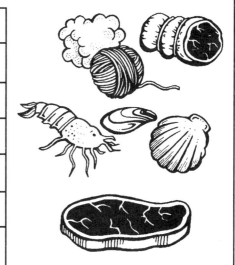

Extension activities (delete before photocopying or leave as instructions for parents or carers).
A. Ask the children if they remember the names of the objects. They should fill in the missing letters to make the words.
B. The children should find out from the book what is produced on each type of farm and present this information in a different way – by drawing lines to link them. Ask the children to draw and label two animals that are each kept for two purposes. They should notice that sheep are kept for both wool and meat and cows are kept for both milk and meat.

Fast Food

A What did they eat? ✔

	fishburger	hamburger	hot dog
Jake			
Pete			
Sam			
Maria			
Uncle Joe			

B Fill in the missing words.

Maria did not want a _____ ,

a _____ or a _____ .

She wanted _____ .

ice cream
hamburger
hot dog
fishburger

Extension activities (delete before photocopying or leave as instructions for parents or carers).
A. This activity encourages the children to read the book to find information which they then present on the chart.
B. · The children fill in the missing words to show what Maria wanted and did not want.
On the back of the sheet the children could draw Maria with her food. Ask them why she had nothing to eat.

Moving In

A Fill in the missing names.

Sharma   Patch   Jake   Dad
Sam   Tabby   Tommy   Grandma

B Fill in the missing letters. Use the pictures to help.

1.	t	r		c	k		
2.	c	h				r	e	n
3.	b		d				
4.	c					r	
5.	t			l	e		
6.	T			b	y		
7.	c			e			

Extension activities (delete before photocopying or leave as instructions for parents or carers).
A. The activity focuses on the characters whom the children have met in this and other books. The activity reinforces their names and develops the skill of labelling.
B. The pictures show objects in the story. The children should finish the words and then read them.
Write the sentence 'Here are the men carrying the bed.' Ask the children to copy it and to draw a picture to show what it says.

Our Cat

A Fill in the missing words.

	We have a big, _____ cat at home.	blue brown black
	He likes to eat _____ .	fish figs fruit
	He likes to drink _____ .	melon milk malt

B | Yes | or | No |

	I painted a picture of our cat.	
	My brother cried.	
	My sister laughed.	
	I laughed.	
	Dad gave me a hug.	

Extension activities (delete before photocopying or leave as instructions for parents or carers).

A. The activity encourages the children to look at the book to find out what the cat is like and what he likes to eat and drink. They should fill in the missing words.

B. The children should write 'Yes' or 'No' to show what happened in the story. Ask them to draw and label all the people and animals in the story. Introduce the word 'characters' to describe them.

Jimmy

A What can Jimmy do? ✔ or ✗

run ☐   jump ☐

hear ☐   write ☐

read ☐   paint ☐

play football ☐

B Fill in the missing words.

	Jimmy hears with his _____ .	lips ears eyes hands
	He looks at Dad's _____ and he looks at Dad's _____ .	nose lips eyes hands ears
	Jimmy _____ with his lips and with his hands.	smells hears talks sees

Extension activities (delete before photocopying or leave as instructions for parents or carers).
A. The children should check in the book to find out what Jimmy can do. They present this information in the form of a chart, ticking the things that Jimmy can do and putting a cross by anything he cannot do.
B. When the children have filled in the missing words they could read the sentences. This is an opportunity to present people with disabilities in a positive way. Jimmy cannot hear, but he can do many other things.

A Visit to the Library

A Join the children to the books.

Tammy   Lee   Sam   Nicole   Brent   Mandy   Tony

B Fill in the missing words.

librarian   children   stamps   book   library

The children are in the _____ .

They take their books to the _____ .

She _____ them.

She says, "Which _____ should I read?"

All the _____ say, "Mine!"

Extension activities (delete before photocopying or leave as instructions for parents or carers).

A. The children should use the book to check which character is which and to find out which books they chose from the library. They should draw lines to join the characters to their books.

B. The book will help the children to fill in the missing words. Ask them to read the sentences they have completed. Write the sentence: 'The librarian stamps the books.' The children could copy and illustrate it.

Playing with Dad

A Fill in the missing words.

| looked for them | hide and seek | hid |

Dad, Tommy and Sam played _____ .

Tommy and Sam _____ .

Dad _____ .

B Where could they hide?
Draw the pictures and fill in the missing words.

Under the _____	In the _____
Where did Dad find them?	
_____	

Extension activities (delete before photocopying or leave as instructions for parents or carers).
A. The children should refer to the story to remind themselves of what happened. Ask them to fill in the missing words then read the sentences.
B. This reinforces the positional words 'under' and 'in'. The children should draw the places where Tommy and Sam thought of hiding and write the missing words.
Ask the children to draw a picture of where they play hide and seek. They could give the picture a caption.

Getting Ready for School

A Where was it? Join the words to the pictures.

on the bed

in the school bag

in the bowl

in the cupboard

on the table

in Mark's room

B Finish the sentences.

where it should be

where it shouldn't be

Mark's school bag was _____ .

His book was _____ .

His lunch box was _____ .

His apple was _____ .

His sweatshirt was _____ .

The dog was _____ .

Extension activities (delete before photocopying or leave as instructions for parents or carers).
A. The children should refer to the book to find out where each lost item was found and then draw lines to join the things to the places where they were. The activity reinforces positional language such as 'in' and 'on'.
B. The activity focuses on repeated language in the story, 'where it should be' and then the unexpected 'where it shouldn't be'. The pictures could be copied and cut out for the children to show the order they were looked for.

I Know That Tune!

A Label the instruments and join them to the people.

> guitar   banjo   recorder
> trumpet   violin   flute

the truck driver

the shop keeper

Grandma

Katy

the rubbish collector

Dad

Extension activities (delete before photocopying or leave as instructions for parents or carers).

A. The activity reinforces the names of the instruments shown in the story. The children should copy them into the right boxes then draw lines to join the instruments to the people who played them. They could refer to the story to find out.

Ask the children what the tune was. They could draw a picture to show what the tune was and give it a caption.

The Car Accident

A Write the correct sentence under each picture.

| The police officer came. | Dad stopped the car. |
| The man in the yellow car went to the panel beater. | The yellow car went into the back of Dad's car. |

Extension activities (delete before photocopying or leave as instructions for parents or carers).
A. The children need to look closely at the pictures and find them in the book. They then should match the text on this page to that in the book, before copying it under the right pictures.
Ask the children to draw some traffic lights on red. They should add the cars. Help them to find out what other colours traffic lights have. They could draw them and draw the cars. Their drawings should show whether the cars are moving, stopping or starting.

Dogs

A Join the dogs to what they do.

Farm dogs

Police dogs

Hunting dogs

Drug-sniffing dogs

Guard dogs

Show dogs

find a bird.

win prizes.

sniff the cargo to find drugs.

guard the factory at night.

help the police officer catch the thief.

round up sheep.

B Which dogs are found in these places?

Factory _____   Hills _____

Dog show _____   Airport _____

Farm _____   _____

Extension activities (delete before photocopying or leave as instructions for parents or carers).
A.   Ask the children what work the dogs in the story do. They should draw lines to join the dogs to what they do and then read the sentences they have made.
B.   The children use the information from A to show the work of the dogs in the places described. Ask the children if they can remember the name of the other kind of dog in the book and what it does. They should write this in the spaces.

The Bird Barn

A What colour are they? ✔

	blue	green	brown	red	yellow	orange	white
canaries							
lovebirds							
finches							
parrot							
budgies							

B Fill in the missing words.

My _____ and I
looked at the pet birds.

"I like the _____ ,"
said my brother.

"I like the _____ ," I said.

The _____ had a yellow crest.

We got some _____ .

budgies

lovebirds

brother

canaries

parrot

Extension activities (delete before photocopying or leave as instructions for parents or carers).
A. The activity reinforces words for colours. Help the children to make their own charts to show the colours of other familiar pets, such as cats, dogs, goldfish, hamsters and gerbils.
B. The children should use the book to find the missing words, by matching them to those in the box.
Ask the children to draw another kind of bird that can be kept as a pet. They could label it.

Lizard

A Where was the lizard? ✔ or ✘

The lizard slid under the

rubbish bins	
wood	
yellow boot	
shed door	

The lizard slid into the

rubbish bins	
wood	
yellow boot	
shed door	

The lizard slid behind the

rubbish bins	
wood	
yellow boot	
shed door	

B Fill in the missing words.

snake	lizard	So I see	yard

The lizard slid out of the _____ .

She saw a _____ .

"Snake," said the _____ , "They are looking

for you."

" _____ ," said the snake.

The Astronauts

A Write the correct word in each box.

helmet   Maria   Pete   space suit   spaceship

B Fill in the missing words.

	Pete and Maria are going into _____ .	the sea space the cave
	"Look out! Look out!" _____ Pete. "Here comes a UFO!"	yelled whispered asked
	"We have crashed ____ _____ !"	on Earth at night in space

Extension activities (delete before photocopying or leave as instructions for parents or carers).
A.   The activity requires the children to find information in the story and to use it in a different way. It develops the skill of labelling.
B.   The children should find the pictures shown on this page in their book and find the words that are missing. They could draw Pete with a speech bubble and write what they think he would say as the spaceship is about to be launched.

The Storm

A Write the words in the correct order.

The lightning flashes.

The clouds rush across the sky.

We sit on the step and watch.

The rain starts.

The thunder rumbles.

The wind blows.

It rains and it rains and it rains.

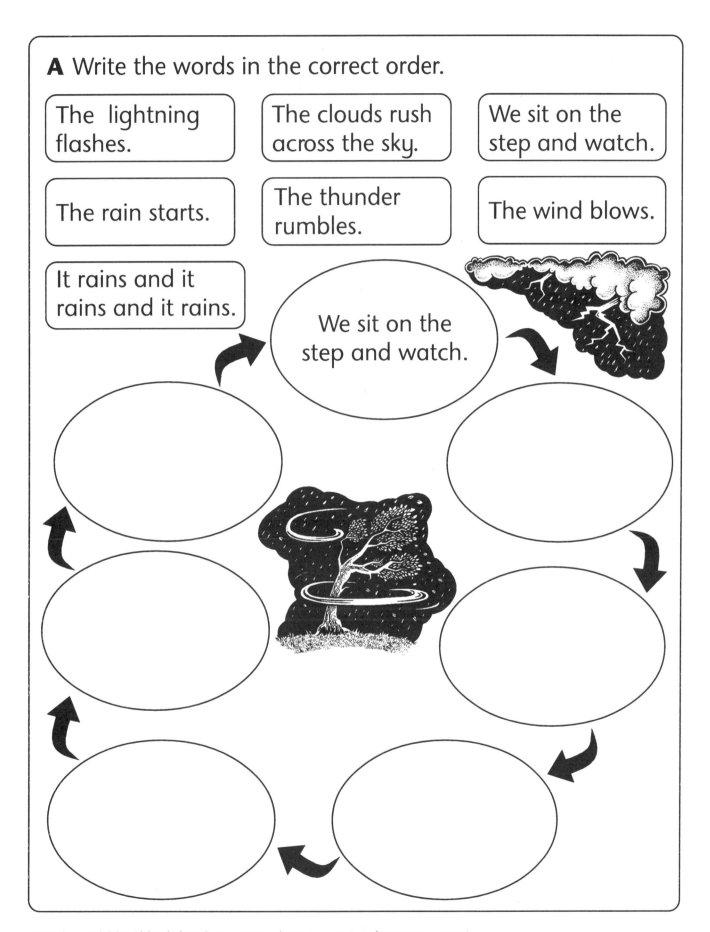

We sit on the step and watch.

Three Muddy Monkeys

A Write what they said in the speech bubbles.

> Let's go home and get some lunch.
> We are muddy monkeys.   Monster monkeys!

Three silly monkeys were playing in the mud.

They lay down on the grass.

The other monkeys were frightened.

B Fill in the missing words.

"Oh, no!" said the _____ silly monkey.

"Monster monkeys!" said the _____

silly monkey.

"RUN!" said the _____ silly monkey.

second

third

first

Extension activities (delete before photocopying or leave as instructions for parents or carers).
A. The children should look for the pictures shown here in the story book. They can then find the correct words to copy into the speech bubbles. Draw their attention to the speech bubbles in the book.
B. Ask the children to find the part of the book where the muddy monkeys look in the water and make a mistake. The children could explain why the silly muddy monkeys went home.

The Roller Blades

A Fill in the missing letters. Use the pictures to help.

1.   2.   3.   4.

1.	r		l	l		■		b	l				
2.	C				s				
3.	h		l	m	
4.	J			u	
5.	t				

5.

B Write the words in the correct order.

roller I blades. my like

I like _____

my will I see go friend. to

I will go _____

helmet on. your Put

Put your _____

tree! Look for out the

Look out _____

Extension activities (delete before photocopying or leave as instructions for parents or carers).
A. In this activity the children learn to write one letter per square of a puzzle. They should use the pictures to find the pages on which the words appear in the book.
B. Encourage the children to look for the word beginning with a capital letter. This has to be the first word of the sentence. Ask them to identify the last word of the sentence by looking for the one followed by a full stop.

Washing

A Fill in the missing letters.

1. Who put the clothes in?
2. Who put the soap in?
3. Who put the money in?
4. Where did they go next?
5. What did they buy?

1.	P						
2.		i	d				
3.			a				
4.		s	h				
5.			c		■	c	r

B What colour was it? ✔

	white	pink	yellow
Dad's ice cream			
Aidan's ice cream			
Pat's ice cream			
Dad's shirt			
Aidan's socks			
Pat's T-shirt			

What colour were most things? _____

Extension activities (delete before photocopying or leave as instructions for parents or carers).
A. The children should use the book to find the answers to the questions. They could write and draw their own descriptions of a familiar event such as going to the launderette or supermarket, then ask each other questions of the same kind as those at the top of the page.
B. The children should use the book to remind themselves of the colours of the clothes that were washed (not the clothes the characters were wearing). The activity develops the skill of finding information from a book and then presenting it in a different way.

A Trip to the Video Store

A Fill in the missing words.

> space   sport   animals

I am looking for a video on _____ .

I am looking for a video on _____ .

I am looking for a video on _____ .

B Finish the sentences.

Pete and Jake would not let Maria help them because

_____ .

They told her to _____

_____ .

She helped _____ .

Extension activities (delete before photocopying or leave as instructions for parents or carers).
A. The children should use the book to find out what sort of video each character was looking for.
B. Ask them to explain why the others would not let Maria help. The children could describe a time when they have been in a similar situation. Ask them how Maria felt when Jake and Pete told her to go away, and then when Uncle Joe said that she could help him choose a video.

Learning New Things

A Write the names in each box.

Musa   Kim   Brad   Anna

B What did all the mums and dads say?

Extension activities (delete before photocopying or leave as instructions for parents or carers).

A. The children should name the characters from the book. They could describe one character to a partner, who must then guess who it is. Ask them what is special about each character.

B. Ask the children what all the mums and dads said to their children when they were learning new things. The activity develops the skill of recognising speech in text. They could draw something that they have learned to do and write how they felt when they learned it.

What Is It?

A Write the words in the correct places.

| cat | ladybird | spider | wasp |

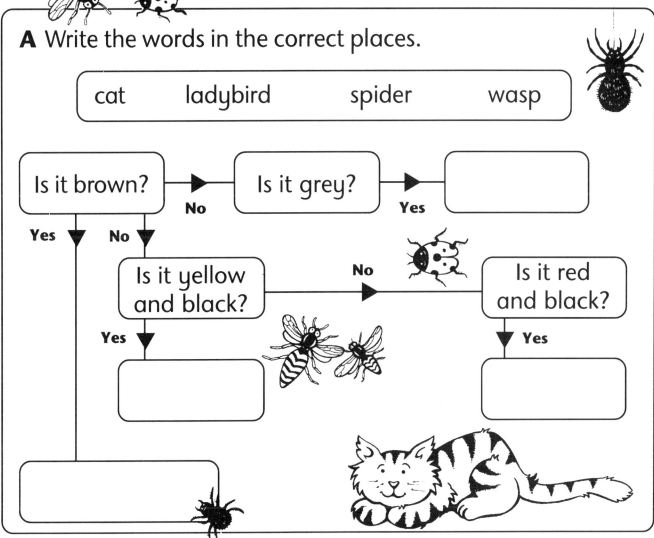

Is it brown? → **No** → Is it grey? → **Yes** → [ ]

Yes / **No**

Is it yellow and black? → **No** → Is it red and black?

Yes → [ ]

Yes → [ ]

[ ]

B Join the words to the pictures.

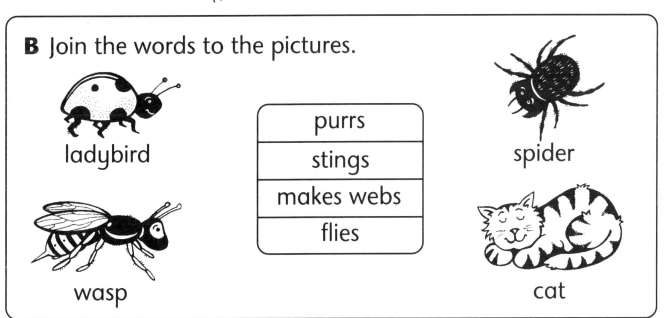

ladybird

| purrs |
| stings |
| makes webs |
| flies |

spider

wasp

cat

Extension activities (delete before photocopying or leave as instructions for parents or carers).
A. This activity introduces simple branching keys. The children may need to use the book to complete it. Provide pictures of four animals, such as a zebra, lion, giraffe and elephant and record on cards the questions that the children ask about them. Arrange the cards on a large sheet of paper, linked with arrows to make a branching key.
B. The children should use the book to find out what the animals do.

FOUNDATIONS FOR READING – *Homework Activities for Early Readers*

Green Plants

A Join the food to the plant it comes from.

tomatoes

soup

salad

lettuce

corn on the cob

potatoes

corn

mashed potato

carrots

cake

B What do they grow?
What do they make?

Bob Green

Pat Green

grows	grows
makes	makes

Extension activities (delete before photocopying or leave as instructions for parents or carers).
A. Ask the children to name the plants in the pictures. They should use the book to find out what can be made from them.
B. Ask the children to use the pictures to find the pages in the book that tell them what Bob and Pat Green grow and make. The activity requires them to transfer this information on to a chart. They could draw and label two more foods that come from green plants.

My Old Cat and the Computer

A Write the correct sentence under each picture.

| He goes to sleep. | He plays with my keyboard. |
| I print his letters. | He types some letters. |

B Fill in the missing words.

The little girl _____ .

Her old cat _____ onto her lap

and starts to _____ .

purr
types
jumps

Extension activities (delete before photocopying or leave as instructions for parents or carers).
A. The children should find the pictures in the book. Ask them what is happening in each picture, then ask them to copy the sentences under the right pictures.
B. When the children have filled in the missing words, ask them to read the finished sentences to see if they make sense. The children could find out from the book what letters the cat typed and draw them on a computer screen.

My Birthday Surprise

A Finish the sentences.

> in the kitchen.   behind the television.

> in your playhouse.   under your bed.

Go and look behind the

_____

Go and look under your

_____

Go and look in your

_____

Go and look in the

_____

B Join the pictures to where each was found.

behind the TV		under the table
under the bed		in the garden
in the playhouse		in the kitchen

Extension activities (delete before photocopying or leave as instructions for parents or carers).

A. The children should find the characters in the book, using the pictures. Ask them where each character told the little girl to look and when they think she could guess what the surprise would be.

B. The children should check the book to find out where each item was found.
Ask them to plan a birthday surprise like this for someone they know. Presents could include sports equipment, a horse and so on. They could think about where they would hide each item.

FOUNDATIONS FOR READING – *Homework Activities for Early Readers*   © Folens (copiable page)

Grandma's Present

A Join the people to what they said.

Dad

Grandma

Thank you for helping me today.

Grandma Wilson helped us today, too.

Can we get her a present for helping us?

Sam

Where are the flowers?

Sharma

We will look after the plant and the flowers will come.

Grandma, come and look in the garden!

Tommy

Jake

B Fill in the missing words.

Dad, Sam and Tommy have a new _____ .	bike car home
Grandma's present was a _____ .	plant garden flower
Grandma's birthday was on _____ .	Monday Saturday Friday

Extension activities (delete before photocopying or leave as instructions for parents or carers).
A. The children should look in the book to find out what each character said. Draw their attention to speech marks.
B. The activity requires the children to use text to find information. Ask them to check each others' answers using the book. They could draw Grandma's present.

Mother Hippopotamus's Dry Skin

A Write what they said in the speech bubbles.

Go to the shop and get some cream in a tube.

Make a mud pack and put it on your face.

My skin feels dry.

Go to the shop and get some cream in a pot.

B Join the words to make the sentences.

The cream in the pot	was no good.
The cream in the tube	was good.
The mud pack	was no good.

The New Nest

A Fill in the missing words.

| roof   nest   make   eggs |

"We must make a new _____ ,"
said Mother Bird.
"It is time to lay my _____ ."
"We will _____ a nest in this
_____ ," said Father Bird.

B Where did they find them? Join the words with lines.

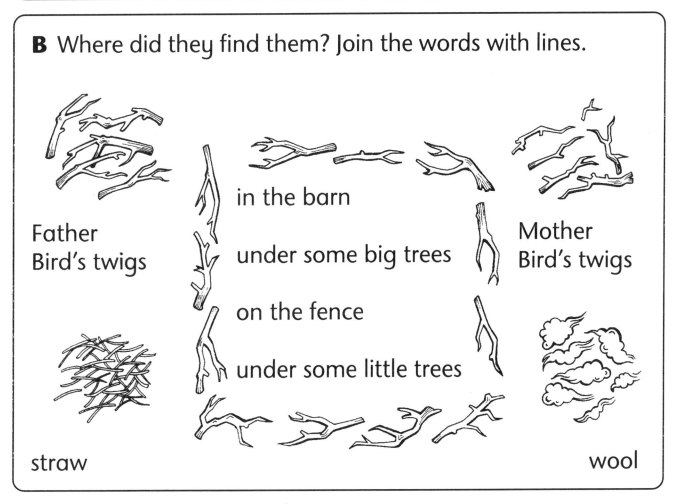

Father
Bird's twigs

in the barn

under some big trees

on the fence

under some little trees

Mother
Bird's twigs

straw

wool

Extension activities (delete before photocopying or leave as instructions for parents or carers).
A. The children should read the sentences and decide which words make sense when used in the gaps. They may be able to do this without reference to the book.
B. Ask the children where the birds found the things to build their nests – they should use the book to find out. Encourage them to use the pictures to find the pages that will tell them this; they could draw a picture map to show where the birds found everything.

Pancakes

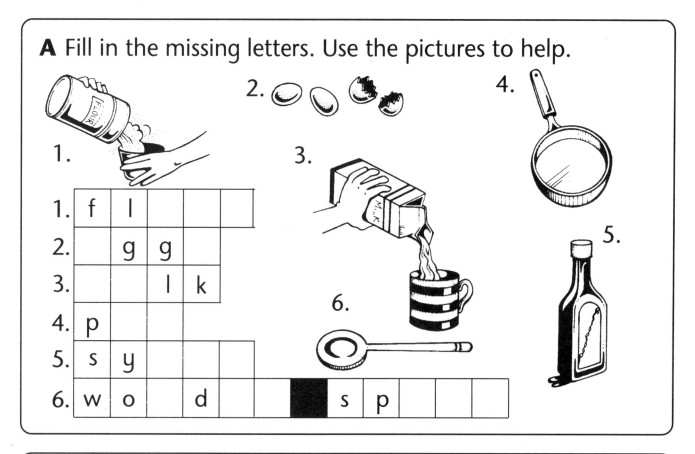

A Fill in the missing letters. Use the pictures to help.

1.	f	l					
2.		g	g				
3.			l	k			
4.	p						
5.	s	y					
6.	w	o		d		▮	s	p			

B Write the words in the correct order.

the flipped pancake. She

She _____

up went over. and It

It went _____

tried Jimmy the pancake. to flip

Jimmy _____

did up. The pancake not go

The pancake did _____

Extension activities (delete before photocopying or leave as instructions for parents or carers).
A. The children should find the pictures in the book. This will help them to find the place in the book where they can find the words.
B. Encourage the children to look for the word that begins with a capital letter – this gives them the first word of the sentence. Draw attention to the full stop. The children could draw and write a pancake recipe using the book; introduce them to the word 'ingredients' and point out that the quantity of each ingredient is missing.

Watching TV

A Finish the sentences.

after school   at school   before breakfast

	Justin watches TV _____ .
	He watches TV _____ .
	He watches TV _____ every day.

B What does Justin hear? ✔ or ✗

Dad when he calls him to get ready for school. ☐

His teacher when he asks him a question. ☐

His sister when she calls him for dinner. ☐

Extension activities (delete before photocopying or leave as instructions for parents or carers).
A. The children should use the book to find out all the times when Justin watches TV. Ask them to read the completed sentences.
B. Ask them to explain why he does not hear people and why he hears some things and not others. They could draw Justin's friends, with speech bubbles to show what they are saying.

Three Silly Monkeys

A Fill in the missing words.

Look at Crocodile. He is asleep in the _____.

We can _____ here.

Crocodile is _____. We can play in the _____.

I am not _____ .

play

jump

Crocodile

swim

river

asleep

beach

big

silly

B Fill in the missing words.

There were _____ silly monkeys.	teeth
The monkeys were _____ .	three
Crocodile had big _____ .	silly

Extension activities (delete before photocopying or leave as instructions for parents or carers).
A. The children should use the book to find out what the silly monkeys and the crocodile said. They should decide which of the words in the box to use to complete the speech bubbles.
B. This activity develops the skill of recognising speech in text. Ask the children to read their completed sentences to see if they make sense. They could write a story of their own using speech bubbles and pictures.

Fun in the Mud

A Fill in the missing names.

_____ woke first.	Karyn Tania Paul
_____ woke up Tania.	Karyn Tania Paul
_____ and _____ went to wake up Karyn.	Karyn Tania Paul

B Fill in the missing letters. Use the pictures to help.

Extension activities (delete before photocopying or leave as instructions for parents or carers).
A. Encourage the children to use the book to find the sequence in which the children woke up. They could draw the three pictures that show which children were awake at each stage.
B. The children should find the pictures in the story – this will help them to locate the words that they need to fill the gaps. Ask them what they think about mud, whether they would play in it and why.

The Baby at Our House

A Fill in the missing words.

	The baby's name is _____ .	Danny Tanya Brett Brooke
	The baby is a _____ .	boy girl
	In the car the baby _____ .	cries laughs sleeps
	Mum is going to bring the baby to _____ on Friday.	work school town

B | Yes | or | No |

Brett's baby brother is called Ryan. ☐

Brooke sleeps a lot. ☐

Brooke laughs a lot. ☐

Dad drives the children to school. ☐

Mum will bath the baby in school. ☐

Extension activities (delete before photocopying or leave as instructions for parents or carers).

A. The children should find in the book the information needed to complete the sentences. Ask them to read the finished sentences to a partner to see if they agree.

B. This encourages the children to re-read the book. Ask them to answer the questions from memory and then check their answers. They could draw a baby they know, write the baby's name and what the baby does.

What Am I?

A Fill in the missing words.

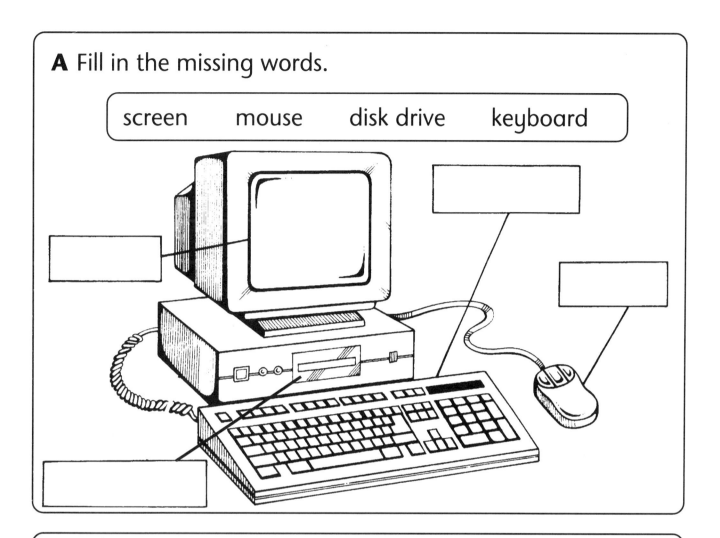

screen	mouse	disk drive	keyboard

B Join the sentences to the words.

You can type on it.	screen
You can use it to move things around.	disk drive
You can store information on it.	mouse
You can use it to see everything you type or draw.	keyboard

Good Sports

A Fill in the missing words.

	The children were playing _____ .	football school skating
	The boys and girls in Mrs Brown's class score a _____ .	game goal ground
	Mrs Brown's class has _____ goals. We have _____ goal.	one three two
	Mrs Brown's class _____ up and down.	walks kicks jumps

B Join the correct words to each class.

the winners		the best players
the losers	our class	the best sports
two goals	Mrs Brown's class	one goal

our class

Mrs Brown's class

Extension activities (delete before photocopying or leave as instructions for parents or carers).
A. The children need to re-read the book to finish the sentences.
B. This activity encourages the children to find information from the text and present it using the diagram provided. They could draw and write about a football match that they have been to.

After School

A Join each sentence to the correct person.

Mum   **Dad**   **Kristen**

Looks after us when we get home from school.

Works in an office.

Works in a shop.

B Fill in the missing words.

Kristen made some _____ for the children.	salad sandwiches soup
They went to the _____ .	park pictures post office
Mum and Dad came home at _____ o'clock.	six seven five
They _____ the children.	saw watched kissed

Extension activities (delete before photocopying or leave as instructions for parents or carers).
A. The children should recognise the characters from the story. Ask them to re-read the book to find out what each one does.
B. Ask the children what happened after school in the book – they may need to check. Ask them to read the finished sentences.
    The children could draw and write about what they do after school and present this as pictures with captions, as in part A.

Too Late!

A Join the animals to the things they travelled on.

Snail

bike

balloons

Bear

truck

Rabbit

car

Hippo

B Write what they said in the speech bubbles.

Can I come too?
No. You will be too late.
You are too late.

Extension activities (delete before photocopying or leave as instructions for parents or carers).

A. The children should check in the book to find out how each character travelled. Ask the children what present each character was taking to the party.

B. The children should read the sentences then copy them into the right speech bubbles. The activity develops the skill of recognising speech in text. Ask the children whose party it was and who was late.

Maria Goes to School

A Fill in the missing words.

Jake goes to _____ .	work school town
Sharma cannot go to school. She is too _____ .	little big old
Tomorrow Maria starts _____ .	school work play

B Join the questions to the picture answers.

Who will be my teacher?

Where will I put my coat?

Where will I put my bag?

Where will I eat my lunch?

Where will I play?

Extension activities (delete before photocopying or leave as instructions for parents or carers).
A. The children should use the book to find the information that they need.
B. Ask the children to read Maria's questions. They could check the answers in the story. Ask them if they can remember their first day at school – they could describe some of the things that they wanted to know about. The children could answer Maria's questions as if she was going to their school and draw and label some instructions for someone who is new to their school.

Going to School

A Fill in the missing words.

Mrs Sharp	**Dusty**	**ducks**
Scamp	**Molly**	**Curly**

Hello, _____ .
I can't stop.

Go back, _____ .
You can't come
with me.

Oh, no, _____ .
I don't have time
to milk you.

Sorry, little _____ !
No food for you now.

Hello, _____ .
I can't stop to give
you a pat.

Hello, _____ .
Thanks for waiting.

B Fill in the missing words.

"Here's your _____ ," said Mum. "Hurry, or you'll miss the _____ ."	bus gates lunch
"No, Mum, I won't forget to shut the _____ ."	lunch bus gates

Extension activities (delete before photocopying or leave as instructions for parents or carers).
A. The children should read what they have written in the speech bubbles. They may need to re-read the book. They could write in speech bubbles some of the things they might say to people or animals on their way to school.
B. The children could complete this without referring to the book, then read their work and decide whether or not each sentence makes sense. Ask the children to draw and label the animals who went to the bus stop.

Tyres

A Write the words in the correct box.

digger   lorries   toys   tractors
wheelbarrows   shopping trolleys

big tyres	little tyres

B Fill in the missing words.

	Some people use old tyres to make _____ .	swings schools sweets
	Some people use old tyres to make _____ .	garages green gardens
	Some of the tyres are under the climbing _____ .	frame field fall
	Some of the tyres are around the _____ .	tyres trees trains

Extension activities (delete before photocopying or leave as instructions for parents or carers).
A. Ask the children to name some uses for old tyres. You could make cards showing each use. Ask the children to sort them into 'uses for big tyres' and 'uses for little tyres' before they fill in the chart.
B. The children should use the book to find the missing words. Ask the children to draw and label something that they would like to make from old tyres.

Colours

A Colour in the balloons.

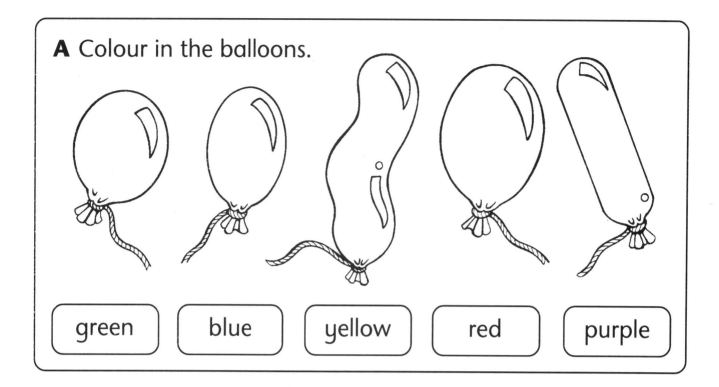

green	blue	yellow	red	purple

B What colour are they? ✔

	green	blue	yellow	red	purple	orange
banana						
pawpaw						
kiwifruit						
plum						
grape						
balloons						
flowers						

Extension activities (delete before photocopying or leave as instructions for parents or carers).
A. This reinforces the words for colours. The children should colour the balloons in the correct colours.
B. The children should find each item in the story and check its colour. The activity develops the skill of finding information in text and presenting it in a different way – as a chart. Help the children to make another chart to show the colours of the fruits and clothes.

Bikes

A Fill in the missing words.

the park	town	school	work

Mum rides her bike to _____ .

Bill rides his bike to _____ .

Jill and Terry ride their bikes to _____ .

I ride my bike to _____ every day.

B Join the correct sentence to each picture.

bike racks

Tools for fixing bikes.

Read about fixing bikes.

I sometimes have to take my bike there.

To keep our bikes safe at school.

library book

bike kit

bike shop

Extension activities (delete before photocopying or leave as instructions for parents or carers).
A. Ask the children where each character goes on his or her bike. They could check in the story.
B. The children should find the pictures in the book. This helps them to locate the information that they need to complete the activity.
   Ask them to explain why some people keep their bikes in their homes.

Fishing

A Write the missing words in the boxes.

| fishing line | hooks | bait | hat |

B Fill in the missing words.

Mum put some _____ on her hook.	fish bite bait
At last, she feels the _____ bite.	bait line fish
"We can't eat a little _____ for dinner!"	crab fish bite
"A _____ !" says Mum. "No more fishing!"	bite boot bait

Mr Bumbleticker Likes to Cook

A Join the friends to the day they came to dinner.

Chinese friends

Italian friends

Monday

Tuesday

Wednesday

Thursday

Friday

Greek friends

Mexican friends

Mrs Bumbleticker

B Fill in the missing words.

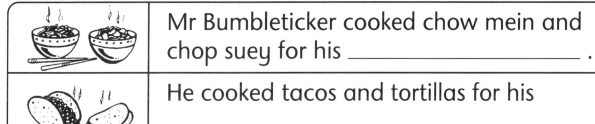

	Mr Bumbleticker cooked chow mein and chop suey for his _____ .
	He cooked tacos and tortillas for his _____ .
	He cooked lasagne and linguine for his _____ .
	He cooked souvlakis and shish kebabs for his _____ .
	He cooked corned beef and cabbage for _____ .

Extension activities (delete before photocopying or leave as instructions for parents or carers).

A. The children could find on a globe or world map the countries of Mr Bumbleticker's friends. They may need to re-read the book to find out on which days they came to dinner.

B. Ask the children if they have tried the foods that Mr Bumbleticker cooked. They could collect pictures of recipes from magazines and choose alternative meals for Mr Bumbleticker's friends. Ask them to draw and label their favourite food.

Marco Saves Grandpa

A Write the correct sentence under each picture.

| Marco looks after Grandpa. | Marco rides his bike. | Grandpa calls, "I am sick." |

| Marco phones for an ambulance. | Grandpa is digging the garden. | Marco runs to Grandpa. |

B What number did Marco ring? _____

Extension activities (delete before photocopying or leave as instructions for parents or carers).

A. The activity focuses on the sequence of the story. The children could look at the pictures and describe what is happening, then find the right words to put under the pictures.

B. Ask the children if they know what number to telephone in an emergency. They could make pictorial/written instructions for making emergency phone calls and draw and write some rules for what to do when someone is ill.

Uncle Carlos's Barbecue

A Join the food to the place.

at the beach

steak

sausages

fish and chips

at the school picnic

at Dad's birthday party

fish

when Uncle Carlos asked us to dinner

B Write what they said in the speech bubbles.

You have burnt the fish.
I'm just learning.

Extension activities (delete before photocopying or leave as instructions for parents or carers).

A. Ask the children what Uncle Carlos cooked and see if they can remember the places where he had barbecues. They could use the book to find out which food he made at each barbecue.

B. The activity develops the skill of recognising speech in text. The children should look for speech marks as they skim the book. Ask the children to draw and label some other foods that they like to have barbecued.

Mum Paints the House

A Write the correct sentence under each picture.

Mum went to the paint shop.	Mum scraped the house with a paint scraper.
Mum got some of the old paint off with sandpaper.	Mum painted the house.

B What colours did Mum paint the house?

_____ and _____

Extension activities (delete before photocopying or leave as instructions for parents or carers).
A. The activity focuses on the sequence of the story. Ask the children to remember the order in which Mum did the jobs. They could draw this as a time line.
B. See if the children remember the colours that Mum used – they may need to look at the book. The children could draw the house after Mum painted it, colouring in the walls and the parts around the windows and doors the correct colours.

Come and See!

A Fill in the missing letters. Use the pictures to help.

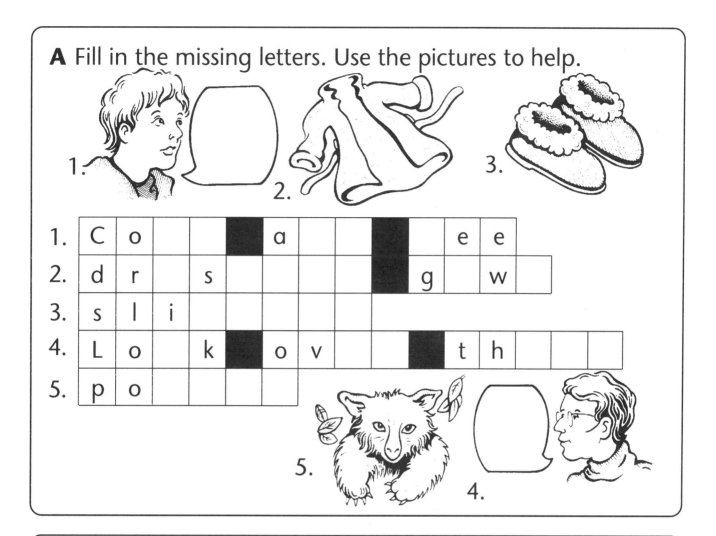

	1	2	3	4	5	6	7	8	9
1.	C	o		■	a			■	e	e
2.	d	r	s					■	g	w
3.	s	l	i							
4.	L	o		k	■	o	v		■	t	h
5.	p	o								

B Fill in the missing words.

The story happened _____ .	in the morning at night in the afternoon
There were _____ children.	six three two
They lived with their _____ .	mum and dad grandpa grandma

Extension activities (delete before photocopying or leave as instructions for parents or carers).

A. The children should find the pages that show the pictures shown here in the book and then find the words. Remind them to write one letter only in each box.

B. Ask the children to complete these sentences without referring to the book. They could then check their answers. Ask them what the children's mum and dad woke them up to see. They could draw it and give it a caption.

The Broken Plate

A Write the correct sentence under each picture.

> They played with the ball.

> Mum took them home.

> The children went to see Grandpa.

> They broke Grandpa's plate.

B Fill in the missing words.

The children were _____ .	angry
	sorry
Mum was _____ .	scared

Extension activities (delete before photocopying or leave as instructions for parents or carers).

A. The children could find in the book the pictures shown here. Ask them what is happening in each picture and see if they can find the words on this sheet that describe what is happening.

B. The children should look at the end of the book to find the missing words. Ask the children to draw the children's faces at the end of the story showing how they felt. They could draw Mum and Grandpa showing how they felt as well.

Women at Work

A Label the pictures. Join each person to where they work.

air traffic controller   conductor   driver
TV camera operator   artist
computer technician   mechanic

concert hall

studio

garage

studio

office

mine

airport

Jimmy's Goal

A Write the correct words in the boxes and colour the picture.

| shoes | shorts | shirt | head | ball | net |

B Fill in the missing words.

Jimmy _____ football.	moan
Big Pete _____ the ball off his head.	watches
The boys and girls are _____ the ball.	bounces
Jimmy _____ the ball.	plays
"Oh, no!" _____ the mums and dads.	kicking

Extension activities (delete before photocopying or leave as instructions for parents or carers).
A. Ask the children to use the book to find out what colours the picture should be. The activity develops the skill of using information given to label and complete a picture.
B. The children should be able to complete this activity without looking at the book. Ask them to read what they have written to see if it makes sense. Ask the children what Jimmy did wrong and what the score in the football match was.

The Rain

A Draw pictures and fill in the missing sentences.

under the table	in the bath
in the chair	in bed

Where did Grandad sleep?

1. 	2.
3.	4.

B Fill in the missing letters.

What did Grandad put under the drip?

1.			t		
2.		o	o		
3.			c	k	

Extension activities (delete before photocopying or leave as instructions for parents or carers).
A. The children may need to re-read the story to find out the order of the places where Grandad slept. They could use the pictures in the book to help them to draw those places, in the right order, from 1 to 4.
B. The children will need to re-read the book to find out what Grandad put under the drip in pictures 1, 2 and 3. Ask them to draw the person who rescued Grandad.

Dad's New Path

A Fill in the missing words.

| little girl   mouse   cat   dog |

First the _____ walked on Dad's new path.

Then the _____ walked on the path.

Then the _____ walked on it.

Dad made the path nice and smooth.

Then, at night the _____ walked on it.

B Join the boxes.

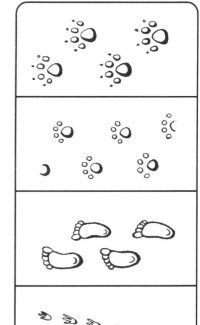

pit pat, pit pat	mouse	
skitter skatter, skitter skatter	little girl	
slip slop, slip slop	cat	
split splat, split splat	dog	

Extension activities (delete before photocopying or leave as instructions for parents or carers).
A. This requires the children to think about the sequence of events in the story.
B. The children should draw lines to link each action to a character and each character to its/her footprints.

FOUNDATIONS FOR READING – *Homework Activities for Early Readers*   © Folens (copiable page)

Insects That Bother Us

A Draw lines to join the beginning and end of the sentences.

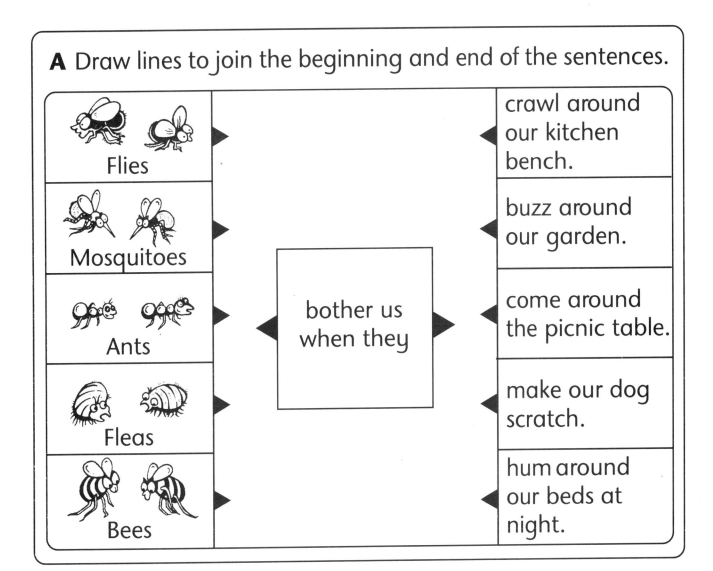

Flies

Mosquitoes

Ants

Fleas

Bees

bother us
when they

crawl around
our kitchen
bench.

buzz around
our garden.

come around
the picnic table.

make our dog
scratch.

hum around
our beds at
night.

B Fill in the missing words.

| mosquitoes | flies | bees | ants | fleas |

We wave our hands to keep _____ away.

We wash the kitchen bench to keep _____ away.

When _____ bother us we find another place to play.

We use powder to keep _____ away from the dog.

We use window screens to keep out _____ .

Extension activities (delete before photocopying or leave as instructions for parents or carers).
A. The children may need to re-read the book to find out which insects bother people in each of the ways listed.
B. They could also re-read the book to check how people deal with insects. Ask the children to draw and label some other insects that bother people.

Baby Elephant's New Bike

A Write the story in the correct order.

> Baby Elephant could ride the bike all by himself.
> He could not ride it.
> Baby Elephant had a new bike.
> Dad helped him. He held the bike.

_____

_____

_____

_____

_____

B Who said it? Draw lines to join the characters to the words.

Baby Elephant

I can't ride this bike!

Yes, you can.
Try again.

I can ride
the bike!

Dad

Extension activities (delete before photocopying or leave as instructions for parents or carers).
A. The activity focuses on the order of the story.
B. This develops the skill for recognising speech in text. The children could use the book to find out which elephant said what.
   Ask the children if it was easy for Baby Elephant to learn to ride the bike and how they know this. They should draw lines to link the
   character to their words.

Making Friends

A Copy from the book what they said in the speech bubbles.

Tyrannosaurus Rex

Tyrannosaurus Rex's mother

B Fill in the missing words.

Tyrannosaurus Rex tried _____ to make friends.	
Then he tried _____ .	Tyrannosaurus Rex
Then he tried _____ .	dinosaurs
	sharing his snack
The other _____ said, "No! Not today."	smiling
His father told him to find another	shaking hands
_____ .	

Extension activities (delete before photocopying or leave as instructions for parents or carers).
A. The children will need to re-read the book to find the three things that Tyrannosaurus Rex's mother told him to do to make friends. They should identify speech in the text by looking for speech marks.
B. When the children have completed the sentences, they could check the sequence in the book. Ask them if these ways of making friends worked and if not why not. They could suggest what they would do to make friends.

Mother Hippopotamus's Hiccups

A Write what they said in the speech bubbles.

> Eat some sugar.

> Rub your ear.

> Hold your breath and count to ten.

> Drink your tea backwards.

B Did it work? | Yes | or | No |

Holding her breath and counting to ten.

Rubbing her ear.

Eating sugar.

Drinking tea backwards.

Getting a fright.

Extension activities (delete before photocopying or leave as instructions for parents or carers).

A. Ask the children to re-read the story to find out what Mother Hippopotamus's friends told her to do to get rid of her hiccups. They should recognise speech by the speech marks.

B. The children write 'yes' or 'no' to show which method got rid of Mother Hippopotamus's hiccups. They could make speech bubbles to show what they would have told her to do and display them next to self-portraits.

Our Baby

A Fill in the missing words.

| grumpy | cries | cot | cheeks | cradle |

The baby is too big for her _____ .

She sleeps in a _____ .

She is _____ because she is getting teeth.

She _____ a lot.

Her _____ get very red.

B Join the correct person to the sentence.

Brooke's mum

Brooke's sister

plays with the baby.

sings to the baby.

reads to the baby.

rocks the baby.

lets the baby play with her dolls.

C What stopped the baby being grumpy?

_____

Extension activities (delete before photocopying or leave as instructions for parents or carers).
A. The children will need to re-read the book to decide in which sentence to write 'cot' and in which to write 'cradle'. They should be able to complete the others without reference to the book.
B. The children should draw lines to join the characters to the things that they do.
   Ask the children what they would do to make Brooke feel happier.

My Friend Trent

A Fill in the missing words.

	Trent was my _____ .	cat brother neighbour
	Every _____ we went to the park.	day weekend Monday
	One day, Trent's mum got a new _____ .	job car dress
	I wrote Trent _____ .	books postcards letters
	We went on the _____ to see Trent.	bus train plane

B Join the picture to the correct word.

| happy | excited | sad |

Extension activities (delete before photocopying or leave as instructions for parents or carers).
A. The children will need to re-read the book to remind themselves of what happened in the story. They should use the pictures shown here to find the pages that they need in the book.
B. Ask the children how the little girl in the story feels in each picture. They should draw lines to join the pictures to the right words.
Ask the children to draw something that they like to do with friends.

The Baseball Game

A Join the correct animal to each sentence.

Little Elephant

Little Lion

pitched the ball.

hit the ball and ran to first base.

hit the ball very hard, up into the air.

looked everywhere but couldn't find the ball.

Little Hippopotamus

Little Monkey

B Finish the sentence.

in the grass.

in the tree.

under Little Hippopotamus.

in the sky.

The ball was _____ .

Extension activities (delete before photocopying or leave as instructions for parents or carers).
A. Encourage the children to look for the pictures shown here in the book. They should then be able to find the words that will help them to find out which animal did what.
B. Ask the children if they remember where the ball was. They could draw a ball game that they play, give the picture a caption and explain how to play the game.

Three Silly Monkeys Go Fishing

A Finish the sentences.

I am going to catch a
_____

I am going to catch a
_____

I am going to catch the
_____
_____

The first silly monkey

The second silly monkey

The third silly monkey

B Yes or No

The silly monkeys caught a fish.

They jumped into the pond.

They saw three silly monkeys in the pond.

They saw a crocodile in the pond.

Extension activities (delete before photocopying or leave as instructions for parents or carers).
A. The children should read the words in the speech bubbles. They may have to re-read the book to find the words that finish their sentences.
B. This could be answered without re-reading. It asks the children to recall events from the story. Ask the children what the silly monkeys really saw and why they couldn't see the other silly monkeys when they jumped into the pond.

Things People Do For Fun

A Fill in the missing words.

	_____ like to jump out of planes.	Surfers
	These people go _____ . They fly on hang-gliders.	Trail bike riders
	_____ ride bucking broncos.	Rodeo riders
	_____ ride waves on surfboards.	Divers
	_____ have fun bouncing over bumpy trails.	Skydivers
	_____ dive down into the sea.	Balloonists
	_____ have fun floating in the sky.	hang-gliding

B What do you do for fun?

_____

_____

Extension activities (delete before photocopying or leave as instructions for parents or carers).

A. The children should use the book to help them fill in the missing words to show which people do each activity.

B. They should write what they do to have fun. Ask the children to draw and label three more things that people do for fun.

Trucks

A Write the correct words in the boxes.

engine   trailer   wheel   tyre   brakes

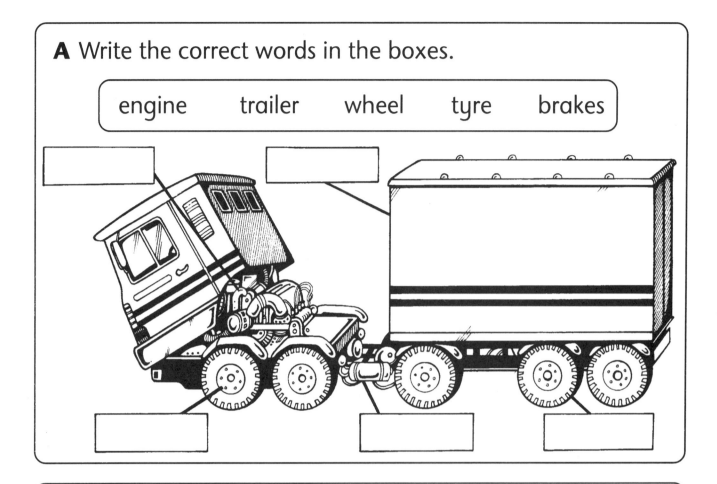

B Fill in the missing words.

Truck engines need _____ fuel to make them run.

They need _____ and _____ to keep them running.

Trucks need good _____ to make them stop safely.

Brakes need _____ to make them work.

_____ need air to make them blast.

horns

water

air

diesel

oil

brakes

Get Lost!

A Write the correct words in the boxes.

| played catch |
| made paper planes |
| played computer games |
| went fishing |

| on the steps. |
| in his bedroom. |
| by the river. |
| in the garden. |

Who?	What?	Where?
Brian		
Eric		
Eric and Brian		
Eric and Brian		

B Finish the sentences.

Annie found her brother

_____.

They _____.

| in his bedroom. |
| in the shed. |
| played skipping. |
| made paper planes. |

Extension activities (delete before photocopying or leave as instructions for parents or carers).
A. The children read the names of the places and the list of things that the children did. They use the book to help them fill in the chart to show what the children were playing and where they were playing.
B. The children draw lines to join the beginnings of the sentences to the right endings. Ask them to read the sentences and check their answers in the book. They could think about why Annie's brother decided to play with her.

Little Monkey Is Stuck

A Write what they said in the speech bubbles.

I can climb up the tree.

I can help you.

Be careful.

B Join the beginnings and endings of the sentences.

Mother Monkey said	helped him.
Little Monkey's tail	frightened.
He yelled	"Help me, help me! I'm stuck in a tree."
He was	"You are only a little monkey."
Big Giraffe	got stuck in a branch.

Extension activities (delete before photocopying or leave as instructions for parents or carers).
A. The children use the book to help them to find out what the characters said. They develop the skill of recognising speech in text by copying the words into the correct speech bubbles.
B. The children need to re-read the book to help them to match the beginnings of the sentences to the right endings.
  Ask the children how Big Giraffe helped Little Monkey.

FOUNDATIONS FOR READING – *Homework Activities for Early Readers*   © Folens (copiable page)

Is It Time Yet?

A Write the correct words in each box.

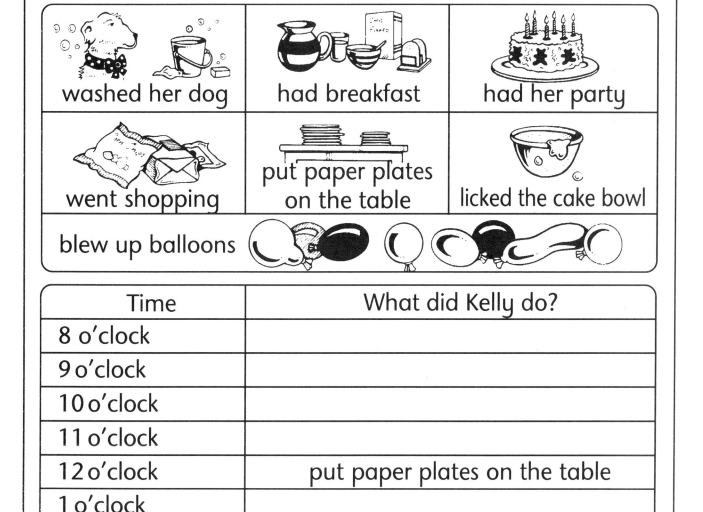

Time	What did Kelly do?
8 o'clock	
9 o'clock	
10 o'clock	
11 o'clock	
12 o'clock	put paper plates on the table
1 o'clock	
2 o'clock	

B Fill in the missing words.

Kelly had breakfast with _____ . She helped _____ put paper plates on the table. She blew up balloons with _____ .	Dad Grandma Mum

Extension activities (delete before photocopying or leave as instructions for parents or carers).
A. The children should look at the pictures and read what Kelly did. They could re-read the book to find out at what time she did each action, putting their answers on the chart.
B. The children should use the book to complete the sentences, finding the answers in the book. They could draw and label Kelly's shopping list.

Lucky We Have an Estate Car

A Join the people to the pictures.

Paul

Karyn

fishing rod

hat

kite

ball

Tania

Mum

B Who opened the gates?
Write the name under the picture.

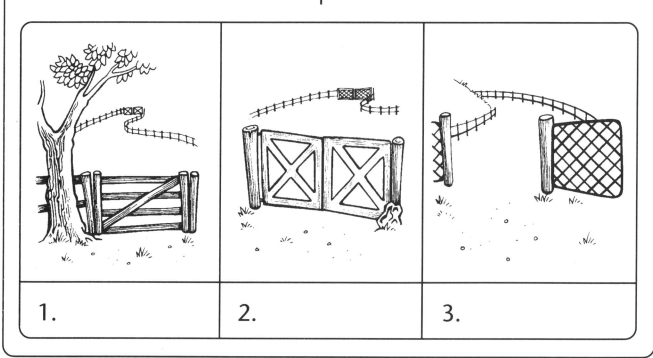

1.

2.

3.

Extension activities (delete before photocopying or leave as instructions for parents or carers).
A. Ask the children if they can remember which characters wanted to put each item in the car. They draw lines to join the people's names to the objects.
B. This requires close observation. All the gates are different, so the children should find them in the book, and then in the boxes write the names of the people who opened them. Ask the children where the family was going.

Mr Bumbleticker Likes to Fix Machines

A Join the words to the right pictures.

big

little

fast

slow

B | Yes | or | No |

The lawnmower needed to be fixed.

The lawnmower ran out of petrol.

Mr Bumbleticker took the handle off the lawnmower.

Mrs Bumbleticker helped him.

Extension activities (delete before photocopying or leave as instructions for parents or carers).
A. The children could complete this without reference to the book. They should look at the pictures and read the words then draw lines to join the words to the right pictures, deciding which machines are big, little, fast and slow.
B. The children use the book to find out which sentences are true. They should write 'Yes' or 'No' in the boxes.
    Ask the children what Mrs Bumbleticker said when she got home.

Silly Willy and Silly Billy

A Write the correct sentences under the pictures.
Draw the missing picture.

Everyone fell into the sea.	Silly Willy went for a swim in the bath.
Six silly workers tried to help.	Silly Billy got his toe stuck in the tap.

Everyone fell

Extension activities (delete before photocopying or leave as instructions for parents or carers).

A. The children could begin by looking at the pictures and finding them in the book. They should find the pictures to copy into the blank boxes and then match the text here to that in the book, copying the correct words under the pictures which show the sequence of the story. Ask the children why Silly Billy put his toe in the tap and how Silly Billy and Silly Willy ended up in the sea.

At the Pet Shop

A Fill in the missing letters. Use the pictures to help.

1.   2.   3.

4.

5.

6.

1.	k		t	t		
2.	p		p	p		
3.	f					
4.	b					
5.	c		c	k		
6.	r		b	b		

B | Yes | or | No |

Chris works in a garage.

He changes the water in the fish tanks once a week.

The cockatoo can talk.

The fish are in a cage.

Extension activities (delete before photocopying or leave as instructions for parents or carers).
A. The children may be able to complete the names of the pets without reference to the book. They write the words in the puzzle and check their answers in the book.
B. Ask the children to read the sentences and check if they are right. They could check their answers in the book.
   Ask the children what Chris in the pet shop does whenever someone buys an animal from him.

Playing Football

A Fill in the missing words.

Football practice is on _____ .	Sundays Tuesdays Saturdays
Joshua's team play on _____ .	Sundays Tuesdays Saturdays
The team is called _____ .	the Lions the Rovers the Tigers

B Colour the right answer.

When Alex scores a goal, what does his dad give him?

a pound

a hug

a present

What did Joshua's dad say he must do if he gives him a pound?

keep it

share it

save it

Extension activities (delete before photocopying or leave as instructions for parents or carers).
A. The children may need to re-read the book to be able to complete the sentences.
B. Ask the children to read the questions. They should colour the right answer in each.
    Ask them whether it was fair for Alex to keep the pound that his dad gave him and if not, why not.

Going to the Hairdresser

A Yes or No

Amber went to the hairdresser with her dad.

Amber had a dry cut.

Amber's mum had a dry cut.

The hairdresser washed Mum's hair.

B Fill in the missing words.

	The hairdresser's name is _____ .	John James Jeremy
	He cut the _____ , the _____ , and the back of Amber's hair.	top front back fringe sides
	The floor was covered with _____ .	dust hair water

Extension activities (delete before photocopying or leave as instructions for parents or carers).
A. The children read the sentences and decide whether or not they are right, writing 'yes' or 'no' in the boxes.
B. The children may need to re-read the book to be able to fill in the missing words.
    Ask the children why Amber and her Mum got their hair cut. They could make a collage of pictures to show the things that hairdressers do to people's hair.

The Best Guess

A What did they do? ✔

	Guess how many jelly beans	Ride on the merry-go-round	Ride on the Ferris wheel
Dad			
Jamie			
Jamie's brother			

B Fill in the missing words.

	The woman had a jar of _____.	stones jelly beans marbles
ONE GUESS 50P	It cost _____ pence to guess how many there were.	fifty twenty thirty
	The woman said, "Come back at _____ o'clock."	three four two
	Dad and the boys had _____ to eat.	hamburgers pies hot dogs
873	Jamie's _____ won the jelly beans.	brother sister dad

Extension activities (delete before photocopying or leave as instructions for parents or carers).
A. The children should try to remember what the characters did at the fair and tick the chart accordingly.
B. The children read the sentences and fill in the missing words. Ask them to read the completed sentences. They could check their answers in the book. Ask them what the best guess was.

Book End

Title

Author(s)

Story book [ ]

Characters

What happened

Information book [ ]

What I learned

Did you like the book? [✔]

Yes, a lot [ ]   Yes, a bit [ ]   No [ ]

Why?

Extension activities (delete before photocopying or leave as instructions for parents or carers).
Copy this page for the children to complete as they finish each book. They should decide what kind of book it is (story or information) in order to fill in the appropriate section of the sheet. Some children may be able to collect the data from the sheets on a database. They could find out which are the most/least popular books and find the answers to questions such as 'Do children in the class like information books or story books better?' and 'Which author do we like best?'

Characters

Pete	Sharma	Maria
Jake	Karyn	Brian
Curtis	Matt	Jim

Extension activities (delete before photocopying or leave as instructions for parents or carers).

Pages 94–96 may be used in various ways:

i) Copy and cut along the dotted lines. Ask the children to group them, in families or by the books they are in.

ii) Play 'Guess Who?' Children play in pairs. Use one or more pages, according to their ability. They each need a copy of the pages to be used. Another copy of each page should be cut as for i). One child takes a character picture from the set. The other asks questions that can be answered by 'Yes' or 'No', to find out which character it is. S/he eliminates characters by covering them with scrap paper. For example, if the answer to 'Is it an animal?' is 'Yes,' cover all the characters that are not animals, and so on.

iii) The children could look for each character in books they have read in the past, including those from the Early band. They could make charts to show which books each character appears in.

Characters

Mr Price

Uncle Joe

Jan

Carlos

Anna

Carmen

Jimmy

Tommy

Sam

Baby Elephant

Brooke

Joshua

Characters

Bobby Green	Kelly	Mr Bumbleticker
Mrs Bumbleticker	Mother Hippopotamus	Mother Lion
Mother Giraffe	Marco	Paul
Paulo	Mandy	Tony

FOUNDATIONS FOR READING – *Homework Activities for Early Readers*

Foundations

Essential Activities for Class or Home

Early Readers

Christine Moorcroft

Folens Publishers

Foundations for Reading Managing Editor: Alison Millar
Editors: Laura Dargie and Andy Brown   Layout artist: Suzanne Ward
Illustrations: Susan Hutchison – Graham-Cameron Illustration, Diana Lamb   Cover design: Kim Ashby
Cover images: Reproduced by kind permission of Lands End Publishing Ltd

© 1997 Folens Limited, on behalf of the author.

Every effort has been made to contact copyright holders of material used in this book. If any have been overlooked, we will be pleased to make any necessary arrangements.

British Library Cataloguing in Publication Data. A catalogue record for this book is available from the British Library.

First published 1997 by Folens Limited, Dunstable and Dublin.
Folens Limited, Albert House, Apex Business Centre, Boscombe Road, Dunstable, LU5 4RL, England.

ISBN 1 86202 277 1

Printed in the United Kingdom by Ashford Colour Press.